MAGNA C

in Salisbury

FREE *adj.* :   not in bondage to or under the control of another; having personal rights and social and political liberty.

Magna Carta is the greatest constitutional document of all times - the foundation of the freedom of the individual against the arbitrary authority of the despot.

Lord Denning, Master of the Rolls 1965

JOHN, by the grace of God King of England, Lord of Ireland, Duke of Normandy and Aquitaine, and Count of Anjou, to his archbishops, bishops, abbots, earls, barons, justices, foresters, sheriffs, stewards, servants, and to all his officials and loyal subjects, Greeting.

KNOW THAT BEFORE GOD, for the health of our soul and those of our ancestors and heirs, to the honour of God, the exaltation of the holy Church, and the better ordering of our kingdom, at the advice of our reverend fathers Stephen, archbishop of Canterbury, primate of all England, and cardinal of the holy Roman Church, henry archbishop of Dublin, William bishop of London, Peter bishop of Winchester, Jocelin bishop of Bath and Glastonbury, hugh bishop of Lincoln, Walter bishop of Worcester, William bishop of Coventry, Benedict bishop of Rochester, Master Pandulf subdeacon and member of the papal household, Brother Aymeric master of the knighthood of the Temple in England, William Marshal earl of Pembroke, William earl of Salisbury, William earl of Warren, William earl of Arundel, Alan de Galloway constable of Scotland, Warin Fitz Gerald, Peter Fitz herbert, hubert de Burgh seneschal of Poitou, hugh de Neville, Matthew Fitz herbert, Thomas Basset, Alan Basset, Philip Daubeny, Robert de Roppeley, John Marshal, John Fitz hugh, and other loyal subjects:

1   FIRST, THAT WE HAVE GRANTED TO GOD, and by this present charter have confirmed for us and our heirs in perpetuity, that the English Church shall be free, and shall have its rights undiminished, and its liberties unimpaired. That we wish this so to be observed, appears from the fact that of our own free will, before the outbreak of the present dispute between us and our barons, we granted and confirmed by charter the freedom of the Church's elections – a right reckoned to be of the greatest necessity and importance to it – and caused this to be confirmed by Pope Innocent III. This freedom we shall observe ourselves, and desire to be observed in good faith by our heirs in perpetuity.

TO ALL FREE MEN OF OUR KINGDOM we have also granted, for us and our heirs for ever, all the liberties written out below, to have and to keep for them and their heirs of us and our heirs:

A Desperate King

In 1214 John was a king in desperate trouble. For the previous 15 years, the reign of this cruel monarch had been an unmitigated disaster. In 1204 he lost Normandy to France, and the year following he fell out with Pope Innocent III by refusing to accept Stephen Langton as Archbishop of Canterbury. The Pope closed England's churches and excommunicated the king.

Equally as important, John had incurred the wrath of the barons From the outset of John's reign, they had suffered under his cruelty and greed. His demands for war funds were excessive, his taxation arbitrary and extortionate, its collection brutal. Defaulters were imprisoned, their lands seized and plundered. There was no redress Something drastic had to happen if civil war was not to break out. That something was Magna Carta.

How could this situation have arisen? The answer lies within the feudal system. Feudalism was the main form of social organisation in medieval Europe, a pyramid based chiefly on land. At its peak was the king; below him came the barons, then lesser gentry and tenants, with the mass of villeins and serfs (types of landless peasant) lowest of all. The commoners at each level of the pyramid had duties and obligations to the people abov and below them. Magna Carta chiefly concerned relations at the top level – between barons and king.

King John hunting, from a 14th-century manuscript. Although keen huntsman, John found himself increasingly preoccupied with the threat of foreign invasion and the opposition of the barons at home.

The English church shall be free, and shall have her rights undiminished and her liberties unimpaired... (Section 1)

By feudal law, the barons held their lands 'in fee' from the mona in return for their sworn loyalty and a commitment to provide the with knights to fight his wars. By the time King John came to the th in 1199, this obligation had been commuted to a cash payment, or 'scutage', which was used to raise an army.

As war was a constant feature of medieval life, soldiers were continually needed. For over a century after the Norman invasion, the kings of England had to fight ever more fiercely to cling on to

> We have granted to all the free men of our kingdom for us and our heirs forever all the liberties written below, to be held by them and their heirs from us and our heirs... (Section 1)

A contemporary manuscript illustration depicting King John being offered a chalice. The portrait shows little of the callousness that John displayed during his reign.

...ossessions in France. Besides this, England, with other Christian ...owers of Europe, for two centuries carried on the Crusades, a ...uccession of costly wars fought to deliver the Holy Land from ...uslim domination.

There were other times when the king was within his rights ... exact money from the barons – national emergencies; the ...arriage of the eldest royal daughter; the succession of an heir ... a baronial title. Even worse, if the heir was not of age, the king ...uld assume the guardianship of the estate, take all the profits ...nd sell off the assets with impunity. Alternatively, he could sell ...e guardianship itself; even the heirs themselves or widows and ...aughters could be sold in marriage!

2   If any earl, baron, or other person that holds lands directly of the Crown, for military service, shall die, and at his death his heir shall be of full age and owe a 'relief', the heir shall have his inheritance on payment of the ancient scale of 'relief'. That is to say, the heir or heirs of an earl shall pay – 100 for the entire earl's barony, the heir or heirs of a knight 100s, at most for the entire knight's 'fee', and any man that owes less shall pay less, in accordance with the ancient usage of 'fees'.

3   But if the heir of such a person is under age and a ward, when he comes of age he shall have his inheritance without 'relief' or fine.

4   The guardian of the land of an heir who is under age shall take from it only reasonable revenues, customary dues, and feudal services. he shall do this without destruction or damage to men or property. If we have given the guardianship of the land to a sheriff, or to any person answerable to us for the revenues, and he commits destruction or damage, we will exact compensation from him, and the land shall be entrusted to two worthy and prudent men of the same 'fee', who shall be answerable to us for the revenues, or to the person to whom we have assigned them. If we have given or sold to anyone the guardianship of such land, and he causes destruction or damage, he shall lose the guardianship of it, and it shall be handed over to two worthy and prudent men of the same 'fee', who shall be similarly answerable to us.

5   For so long as a guardian has guardianship of such land, he shall maintain the houses, parks, fish preserves, ponds, mills, and everything else pertaining to it, from the revenues of the land itself. When the heir comes of age, he shall restore the whole land to him, stocked with plough teams and such implements of husbandry as the season demands and the revenues from the land can reasonably bear.

6   heirs may be given in marriage, but not to someone of lower social standing. Before a marriage takes place, it shall be made known to the heir's next-of-kin.

7   At her husband's death, a widow may have her marriage portion and inheritance at once and without trouble. She shall pay nothing for her dower, marriage portion, or any inheritance that she and her husband held jointly on the day of his death. She may remain in her husband's house for forty days after his death, and within this period her dower shall be assigned to her.

8   No widow shall be compelled to marry, so long as she wishes to remain without a husband. But she must give security that she will not marry without royal consent, if she holds her lands of the Crown, or without the consent of whatever other lord she may hold them of.

The Final Straw

9   Neither we nor our officials will seize any land or rent in payment of a debt, so long as the debtor has movable goods sufficient to discharge the debt. A debtor's sureties shall not be distrained upon so long as the debtor himself can discharge his debt. If, for lack of means, the debtor is unable to discharge his debt, his sureties shall be answerable for it.
If they so desire, they may have the debtor's lands and rents until they have received satisfaction for the debt that they paid for him, unless the debtor can show that he has settled his obligations to them.

10   If anyone who has borrowed a sum of money from Jews dies before the debt has been repaid, his heir shall pay no interest on the debt for so long as he remains under age, irrespective of whom he holds his lands. If such a debt falls into the hands of the Crown, it will take nothing except the principal sum specified in the bond.

11   If a man dies owing money to Jews, his wife may have her dower and pay nothing towards the debt from it. If he leaves children that are under age, their needs may also be provided for on a scale appropriate to the size of his holding of lands. The debt is to be paid out of the residue, reserving the service due to his feudal lords. Debts owed to persons other than Jews are to be dealt with similarly.

12   No 'scutage' or 'aid' may be levied in our kingdom without its general consent, unless it is for the ransom of our person, to make our eldest son a knight, and (once) to marry our eldest daughter. For these purposes only a reasonable 'aid' may be levied. 'Aids' from the city of London are to be treated similarly.

13   The city of London shall enjoy all its ancient liberties and free customs, both by land and by water. We also will and grant that all other cities, boroughs, towns, and ports shall enjoy all their liberties and free customs.

14   To obtain the general consent of the realm for the assessment of an 'aid' – except in the three cases specified above – or a 'scutage', we will cause the archbishops, bishops, abbots, earls, and greater barons to be summoned individually by letter. To those who hold lands directly of us we will cause a general summons to be issued, through the sheriffs and other officials, to come together on a fixed day (of which at least forty days notice shall be given) and at a fixed place. In all letters of summons, the cause of the summons will be stated. When a summons has been issued, the business appointed for the day shall go forward in accordance with the resolution of those present, even if not all those who were summoned have appeared.

Neither we nor our bailiffs shall seize any land or rent in payment of a debt so long as the chattels – items of property – of the debtor are sufficient to repay the debt... (Section 9)

John was not the first English ruler to extort money through the feudal system, but in his reign, abuse of regal power reached new depths. By 1213, the barons were bitter and determined in their opposition to the king. With no allies left at home, threatened with invasion from France and with no obvious way to defend the realm only one course lay open to him – to regain the papal support

he had lost eight years before. The only way he could achieve this was by surrendering England and Ireland to Rome, receiving them back in return for a feudal bond of allegiance, and an annual tribute of 1000 marks (£666). It was abject defeat, but it d bring him back within the Church, protection which John cynical sought to exploit.

We decree and grant that all cities, boroughs, towns and ports sha have all their liberties and free customs... (Section 13)

The final straw for the barons came with John's defeat at Bouvines in July 1214, ending all hope of recapturing Normandy The exactions to fund this debacle had been particularly harsh and now they had lost any chance of a return on their outlay. In January 1215, in full armour, they faced the king in London, demanding a charter confirming the ancient liberties embodied in the coronation oath which John had recently been forced to swear once again. The king stalled for time, saying that it was too complex an issue on which to give an instant response. Instead he arranged to meet them after Easter 1215 at Northampton.

Common pleas shall not follow our court
but shall be in some fixed place... (Section 17)

We shall send two justices through each county four times a year
who shall hold the said assizes in the county court on the day and in
the place of meeting of the county court... (Section 18)

Then, in typically deceitful style, he sent messengers to Rome asking for support. At the same time he took the oaths of a crusader, wearing the cross on his clothes, in this way giving himself and his possessions the Church's protection.

Just before Easter, the barons met at Brackley near Northampton. Here they repeated their demands and gave them in writing to the king's representatives. These reached the king at Wallingford, in Berkshire, at the same time as a reply to John's message arrived from Rome. The Pope urged moderation, possibly suggesting some kind of arbitration. John accepted this but rejected the barons' demand for a charter.

The die was cast. The barons withdrew their feudal allegiance to the king and laid siege to the nearest royal castle, Northampton. Civil War was imminent.

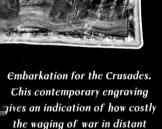

Embarkation for the Crusades. This contemporary engraving gives an indication of how costly the waging of war in distant lands must have been.

15   In future we will allow no one to levy an 'aid' from his free men, except to ransom his person, to make his eldest son a knight, and (once) to marry his eldest daughter. For these purposes only a reasonable 'aid' may be levied.

16   No man shall be forced to perform more service for a knight's 'fee', or other free holding of land, than is due from it.

17   Ordinary lawsuits shall not follow the royal court around, but shall be held in a fixed place.

18   Inquests of novel disseisin, mort d'ancestor, and darrein presentment shall be taken only in their proper county court. We ourselves, or in our absence abroad our chief justice, will send two justices to each county four times a year, and these justices, with four knights of the county elected by the county itself, shall hold the assizes in the county court, on the day and in the place where the court meets.

19   If any assizes cannot be taken on the

Knights on horseback depart for the Crusades. This war to regain the Holy Land from the occupying Muslims was waged for two centuries. The constant demand for money and men to support the campaign was one of the barons' principal grievances.

day of the county court, as many knights and freeholders shall afterwards remain behind, of those who have attended the court, as will suffice for the administration of justice, having regard to the volume of business to be done.

20 For a trivial offence, a free man shall be fined only in proportion to the degree of his offence, and for a serious offence correspondingly, but not so heavily as to deprive him of his livelihood. In the same way, a merchant shall be spared his merchandise, and a husbandman the implements of his husbandry, if they fall upon the mercy of a royal court. None of these fines shall be imposed except by the assessment on oath of reputable men of the neighbourhood.

21 Earls and barons shall be fined only by their equals, and in proportion to the gravity of their offence.

22 A fine imposed upon the lay property of a clerk in holy orders shall be assessed upon the same principles, without reference to the value of his ecclesiastical benefice.

23 No town or person shall be forced to build bridges over rivers except those with an ancient obligation to do so.

24 No sheriff, constable, coroners, or other royal officials are to hold lawsuits that should be held by the royal justices.

25 Every county, hundred, wapentake, and tithing shall remain at its ancient rent, without increase, except the royal demesne manors.

26 If at the death of a man who holds a lay 'fee' of the Crown, a sheriff or royal official produces royal letters patent of summons for a debt due to the Crown, it shall be lawful for them to seize and list movable goods found in the lay 'fee' of the dead man to the value of the debt, as assessed by worthy men. Nothing shall be removed until the whole debt is paid, when the residue shall be given over to the executors to carry out the dead man's will. If no debt is due to the Crown, all the movable goods shall be regarded as the property of the dead man, except the reasonable shares of his wife and children.

27 If a free man dies intestate, his movable goods are to be distributed by his next-of-kin and friends, under the supervision of the Church. The rights of his debtors are to be preserved.

28 No constable or other royal official shall take corn or other movable goods from any man without immediate payment, unless the seller voluntarily offers postponement of this.

29 No constable may compel a knight to pay money for castle-guard if the knight is willing to undertake the guard in person, or with

Runnymede

A free man shall not be amerced (punished) for a trivial offence, except in accordance with the degree of the offence; and for a serious offence he shall be amerced according to its gravity, yet saving always his livelihood ... (Section 20)

A painting from the Houses of Parliament by Charles Sims (1873–1928) illustrating the scene at Runnymede during the negotiations for Magna Carta. While this portrays effectively the hostility and tension of the times, the actual sealing was probably a much less dramatic event.

The barons, having taken the first brave step, were now on the march. Their demands for a charter represented the first time in English history that influential people had combined to make a protest about bad government. John offered arbitration and a promise that they would not be pursued except by law and in court. The barons ignored this, continuing to raise their armies and fortify their castles.

No village or man shall be forced to build bridges at river banks, except those who from of old were legally-bound to do so ... (Section 23)

John tried to buy London's loyalty by granting it a charter. Instead, the city opened its gates to the barons and, with it, the way to the royal exchequer. The king's position became impossible.

A document was drawn up, probably by Archbishop Langton, and full negotiations began in January 1215 in London. They ended in deadlock. Nevertheless, secret talks with the barons

It was in these fields at Runnymede, seven centuries ago, that our forefathers first planted a seed of liberty which helped to spread across the earth the conviction that man should be free and not enslaved.
HM Queen Elizabeth II Runnymede 17 October 1953

...arried on through Langton and the king's chief adviser, William Marshal, Earl of Pembroke. Eventually a deal was struck. It was agreed that the barons, camped at Staines, and the king, resident at Windsor, should come together half way between the two at Runnymede, a field beside the River Thames.

We often get the impression that the meeting was over and done with in one day, 15 June, but this was not so. Tents had been pitched five days before, a prelude to long and intensive negotiations. The outcome of this was The Articles of the Barons, a list of demands, handwritten in Latin, to put before the king. It began 'These are the articles that the barons seek and the king concedes...'.

Let there be one measure of wine throughout our kingdom, and one measure of ale, and one measure of corn ... and one width of cloth. Let it be the same with weights as with measures... (Section 35)

By 15 June the Articles were ready for the king's formal acceptance. On that Monday morning, John arrived with the papal legate, the Archbishop of Canterbury and several other bishops. Someone, probably Langton, read out a summary of the terms. The king declared that he agreed, and his seal was attached to the document.

The event which proved to be such a turning point in England's history was surprisingly brief and lacking in ceremony. In theory, 'a firm and reformed peace' was restored, but once more John's authority was weakened. Few people believed that he would take this lying down. They were proved to be right.

No free man shall be taken or imprisoned or disseised -- have his land taken -- or outlawed or exiled or in any way ruined; nor will we go or send against him, except by the lawful judgement of his peers or by the law of the land. (Section 39)

The feudal system required people at each level of the 'social pyramid' to swear formal allegiance to those above. Here the king receives feudal homage from his vassals. For the barons faced by the intemperance of John's demands and the cruelty of his exactions, such homage became an impossibility.

To no one will we sell, delay or refuse right of justice. (Section 40)

reasonable excuse to supply some other fit man to do it. A knight taken or sent on military service shall be excused from castle-guard for the period of this service.

30 No sheriff, royal official, or other person shall take horses or carts for transport from any free man, without his consent.

31 Neither we nor any royal official will take wood for our castle, or for any other purpose, without the consent of the owner.

32 We will not keep the lands of people convicted of felony in our hand for longer than a year and a day, after which they shall be returned to the lords of the 'fees' concerned.

33 All fish-weirs shall be removed from the Thames, the Medway, and throughout the whole of England, except on the sea coast.

34 The writ called precipe shall not in future be issued to anyone in respect of any holding of land, if a free man could thereby be deprived of the right of trial in his own lord's court.

35 There shall be standard measures of wine, ale, and corn (the London quarter), throughout the kingdom. There shall also be a standard width of dyed cloth, russett, and haberject, namely two ells within the selvedges. Weights are to be standardised similarly.

36 In future nothing shall be paid or accepted for the issue of a writ of inquisition of life or limbs. It shall be given gratis, and not refused.

37 If a man holds land of the Crown by 'fee-farm', 'socage', or 'burgage', and also holds land of someone else for knight's service, we will not have guardianship of his heir, nor of the land that belongs to the other person's 'fee', by virtue of the 'fee-farm', 'socage', or 'burgage', unless the 'fee-farm' owes knight's service. We will not have the guardianship of a man's heir, or of land that he holds of someone else, by reason of any small property that he may hold of the Crown for a service of knives, arrows, or the like.

38 In future no official shall place a man on trial upon his own unsupported statement, without producing credible witnesses to the truth of it.

39 No free man shall be seized or imprisoned, or stripped of his rights or possessions, or outlawed or exiled, or deprived of his standing in any other way, nor will we proceed with force against him, or send others to do so, except by the lawful judgement of his equals or by the law of the land.

40 To no one will we sell, to no one deny or delay right or justice.

41 All merchants may enter or leave England unharmed and without fear, and may stay or travel within it, by land or water, for purposes of trade, free from all illegal exactions,

in accordance with ancient and lawful customs. This, however, does not apply in time of war to merchants from a country that is at war with us. Any such merchants found in our country at the outbreak of war shall be detained without injury to their persons or property, until we or our chief justice have discovered how our own merchants are being treated in the country at war with us. If our own merchants are safe they shall be safe too.

42 In future it shall be lawful for any man to leave and return to our kingdom unharmed and without fear, by land or water, preserving his allegiance to us, except in time of war, for some short period, for the common benefit of the realm. People that have been imprisoned or outlawed in accordance with the law of the land, people from a country that is at war with us, and merchants – who shall be dealt with as stated above – are excepted from this provision.

43 If a man holds lands of any 'escheat' such as the 'honour' of Wallingford, Nottingham, Boulogne, Lancaster, or of other 'escheats' in our hand that are baronies, at his death his heir shall give us only the 'relief' and service that he would have made to the baron, had the barony been in the baron's hand. We will hold the 'escheat' in the same manner as the baron held it.

44 People who live outside the forest need not in future appear before the royal justices of the forest in answer to general summonses, unless they are actually involved in proceedings or are sureties for someone who has been seized for a forest offence.

45 We will appoint as justices, constables, sheriffs, or other officials, only men that know the law of the realm and are minded to keep it well.

46 All barons who have founded abbeys, and have charters of English kings or ancient tenure as evidence of this, may have guardianship of them when there is no abbot, as is their due.

47 All forests that have been created in our reign shall at once be disafforested. River-banks that have been enclosed in our reign shall be treated similarly.

48 All evil customs relating to forests and warrens, foresters, warreners, sheriffs and their servants, or river-banks and their wardens, are at once to be investigated in every county by twelve sworn knights of the county, and within forty days of their enquiry the evil customs are to be abolished completely and irrevocably. But we, or our chief justice if we are not in England, are first to be informed.

49 We will at once return all hostages and charters delivered up to us by Englishmen as security for peace or for loyal service.

50 We will remove completely from their offices the kinsmen of Gerard de Athée, and in future they shall hold no offices in England. The

The Charter Is Written

The Magna Carta, or 'Great Charter', was not what John had set his seal to on 15 June, 1215. The final document was drawn up over the next few days by legal clerks and people of the royal chancery. They reworked the 49 Articles of the Barons into charter form, adding further clauses of wider significance, such as the first one guaranteeing the freedom of the Church. The final total was 63. A council of 25 barons was to supervise the enforcement of Magna Carta, which again was written in Latin, the official language of all documents of the time.

The first full version of Magna Carta was probably ready four days or so after the Articles were sealed. It was written on vellum (fine parchment originating from calfskin) with a seal attached by a separate strip of parchment, but this has broken away in more recent times.

Several copies were needed, to be sent far and wide, and by 24 June seven of these are known to have been ready for distribution. Records tell us that copies were sent to county sheriffs and bishops, but we know the destiny of only thirteen. Three of them went to two bishops while ten were given to Elias of Dereham, Langton's steward, for distribution. It is Elias who provides the link with Salisbury Cathedral. The four originals that survive – two in the British Library, one at Lincoln and one in Salisbury – tell us a great deal. They were written by different people on parchment of different sizes. Details of the wording vary slightly from copy to copy. It is likely then that they were written in haste, and that much bargaining had taken place, for many additions and amendments had made the master text difficult to read.

We will not create justices, constables, sheriffs or bailiffs who do not know the law of the land and mean to observe it well. (Section 45)

Detail from a 13th-century window in Salisbury Cathedral, thought to be contemporary with Magna Carta and to have come from the former cathedral at Old Sarum. It depicts a bishop and a king.

people in question are Engelard de Cigogné, Peter, Guy, and Andrew de Chanceaux, Guy de Cigogné, Geoffrey de Martigny and his brothers, Philip Marc and his brothers, with Geoffrey his nephew, and all their followers.

51 As soon as peace is restored, we will remove from the kingdom all the foreign knights, bowmen, their attendants, and the mercenaries that have come to it, to its harm, with horses and arms.

52 To any man whom we have deprived or dispossessed of lands, castles, liberties, or rights, without the lawful judgement of his equals, we will at once restore these. In cases of dispute the matter shall be resolved by the judgement of the twenty-five barons referred to below in the clause for securing the peace (61). In cases, however, where a man was deprived or dispossessed of something without the lawful judgement of his equals by our father King Henry or our brother King Richard, and it remains in our hands or is held by others under our warranty, we shall have respite for the period commonly allowed to Crusaders, unless a lawsuit had been begun, or an enquiry had been made at our order, before we took the Cross as a Crusader. On our return from the Crusade, or if we abandon it, we will at once render justice in full.

53 We shall have similar respite in rendering justice in connexion with forests that are to be disafforested, or to remain forests, when these were first afforested by our father Henry or our brother Richard; with the guardianship of lands in another person's 'fee', when we have hitherto had this by virtue of a 'fee' held of us for knight's service by a third party; and with abbeys founded in another person's 'fee', in which the lord of the 'fee' claims to own a right. On our return from the Crusade, or if we abandon it, we will at once do full justice to complaints about these matters.

54 No one shall be arrested or imprisoned on the appeal of a woman for the death of any person except her husband.

55 All fines that have been given to us unjustly and against the law of the land, and all fines that we have exacted unjustly, shall be entirely remitted or the matter decided by a majority judgement of the twenty-five barons referred to below in the clause for securing the peace (61) together with Stephen, archbishop of Canterbury, if he can be present, and such others as he wishes to bring with him. If the archbishop cannot be

he Salisbury exemplification measures approximately 4 x 17 inches (36 x 44 cms), d is written on vellum, a fine archment made of calf skin.

The lead seal of King John, attached to authenticate each exemplification.

present, proceedings shall continue without him, provided that if any of the twenty-five barons has been involved in a similar suit himself, his judgement shall be set aside, and someone else chosen and sworn in his place, as a substitute for the single occasion, by the rest of the twenty-five.

56 If we have deprived or dispossessed any Welshmen of lands, liberties, or anything else in England or in Wales, without the lawful judgement of their equals, these are at once to be returned to them. A dispute on this point shall be determined in the Marches by the judgement of equals. English law shall apply to holdings of land in England, Welsh law to those in Wales, and the law of the Marches to those in the Marches. The Welsh shall treat us and ours in the same way.

57 In cases where a Welshman was deprived or dispossessed of anything, without the lawful judgement of his equals, by our father King Henry or our brother King Richard, and it remains in our hands or is held by others under our warranty, we shall have respite for the period commonly allowed to Crusaders, unless a lawsuit had been begun, or an enquiry had been made at our order, before we took the Cross as a Crusader. But on our return from the Crusade, or if we abandon it, we will at once do full justice according to the laws of Wales and the said regions.

58 We will at once return the son of Llywelyn, all Welsh hostages, and the charters delivered to us as security for the peace.

59 With regard to the return of the sisters and hostages of Alexander, king of Scotland, his liberties and his rights, we will treat him in the same way as our other barons of England, unless it appears from the charters that we hold from his father William, formerly king of Scotland, that he should be treated otherwise. This matter shall be resolved by the judgement of his equals in our court.

60 All these customs and liberties that we have granted shall be observed in our kingdom in so far as concerns our own relations with our subjects. Let all men of our kingdom, whether clergy or laymen, observe them similarly in their relations with their own men.

61 SINCE WE HAVE GRANTED ALL THESE THINGS for God, for the better ordering of our kingdom, and to allay the discord that has arisen between us and our barons, and since we desire that they shall be enjoyed in their entirety, with lasting strength, for ever, we give and grant to the barons the following security:

Elias – the Salisbury Connecti

Salisbury's copy of Magna Carta owes its existence to Elias of Dereham. As a young priest, Elias for many years served as steward to two Archbishops of Canterbury, Hubert Walter (1193–1205) and his successor, Stephen Langton (1207–28). Years later he became the canon who for over 20 years was to mastermind the building of Salisbury Cathedral.

Elias was educated, capable and trustworthy, as well as being skilled in the art of negotiation – very much a medieval version of a modern troubleshooter. As Langton's chief secretary, he was at the very heart of the lengthy discussions between king and barons. Records tell us that a 'canon from Dereham' brought to Wallingfor the barons' decision to renounce their allegiance to the king.

As for Magna Carta itself, Elias's status is shown from the fact that he was entrusted to deliver ten of the thirteen copies made – four of the seven prepared at Runnymede, and all six of those written at the follow-up meeting in Oxford a month later.

Strangely, in the light of its later importance, Magna Carta had virtually no immediate effect on relations between barons and kin Civil war rumbled on for two more years. In late 1215, Archbishop Langton went to Rome, leaving Elias in London, stronghold of the rebel barons. He was disgusted at the ruthless way both king and Pope had set aside the charter on which he and others had worked so hard, so he joined the barons in actively seeking to have Prince Louis of France crowned king of England.

All these customs and liberties that we have grante be observed in our kingdom in so far as concerns o relations with our subjects. Let all men of our king whether clergy or laymen, observe them similarly relations with their own men. (Section 60)

Because of this, when war ended in 1217 Elias with Langton, was exempted from the papal amnesty and sent into exile. It took two years befor the Pope would allow him to return and begin his great work at Salisbury.

These events may help to explain why a man of Elias of Dereham's immense ability and experience did not become a bishop, and why no formal monument to him survives. Perhap with the legacy of Salisbury Cathedral and Magna Carta behind him, he needs no other monument.

Two cathedral windows, probably from Old Sarum and in existence at the time of Magna Carta.

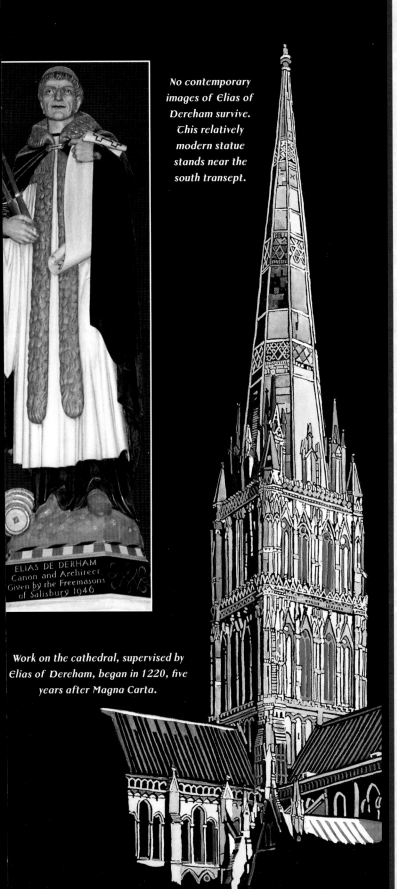

No contemporary images of Elias of Dereham survive. This relatively modern statue stands near the south transept.

ELIAS DE DERHAM
Canon and Architect
Given by the Freemasons
of Salisbury 1946

Work on the cathedral, supervised by Elias of Dereham, began in 1220, five years after Magna Carta.

The barons shall elect twenty-five of their number to keep, and cause to be observed with all their might, the peace and liberties granted and confirmed to them by this charter.

If we, our chief justice, our officials, or any of our servants offend in any respect against any man, or transgress any of the articles of the peace or of this security, and the offence is made known to four of the said twenty-five barons, they shall come to us – or in our absence from the kingdom to the chief justice – to declare it and claim immediate redress. If we, or in our absence abroad the chief justice, make no redress within forty days, reckoning from the day on which the offence was declared to us or to him, the four barons shall refer the matter to the rest of the twenty-five barons, who may distrain upon and assail us in every way possible, with the support of the whole community of the land, by seizing our castles, lands, possessions, or anything else saving only our own person and those of the queen and our children, until they have secured such redress as they have determined upon. Having secured the redress, they may then resume their normal obedience to us.

Any man who so desires may take an oath to obey the commands of the twenty-five barons for the achievement of these ends, and to join with them in assailing us to the utmost of his power. We give public and free permission to take this oath to any man who so desires, and at no time will we prohibit any man from taking it. Indeed, we will compel any of our subjects who are unwilling to take it to wear it at our command.

If one of the twenty-five barons dies or leaves the country, or is prevented in any other way from discharging his duties, the rest of them shall choose another baron in his place, at their discretion, who shall be duly sworn in as they were.

In the event of disagreement among the twenty-five barons on any matter referred to them for decision, the verdict of the majority present shall have the same validity as a unanimous verdict of the whole twenty-five, whether these were all present or some of those summoned were unwilling or unable to appear.

The twenty-five barons shall swear to obey all the above articles faithfully, and shall cause them to be obeyed by others to the best of their power.

We will not seek to procure from anyone, either by our own efforts or those of a third party, anything by which any part of these concessions or liberties might be revoked or diminished. Should such a thing be procured, it shall be null and void and we will at no time make use of it, either ourselves or through a third party.

62 We have remitted and pardoned fully to all men any ill-will, hurt, or grudges that have arisen between us and our subjects,

whether clergy or laymen, since the beginning of the dispute. We have in addition remitted fully, and for our own part have also pardoned, to all clergy and laymen any offences committed as a result of the said dispute between Easter in the sixteenth year of our reign (i.e. 1215) and the restoration of peace.

Magna Carta in Histo

> We hold these truths to be self-evident: that all Men are created equal, that they are endowed by their creator with certain inalienable Rights, that among these are Life, Liberty and the pursuit of happiness – that to secure these Rights, Governments are instituted among Men, deriving their just Powers from the Consent of the Governed.
>
> ## US Declaration of Independence 1776

The men in our kingdom shall have and hold all the aforesaid liberties, rights and concessions well and peacefully, freely and quietly, fully and completely for them and their heirs – in all things and places forever.
(Section 63)

Commemorative plaque in the Abbey Gardens, Bury St Edmunds, near the place where the barons met on 20 November 1214.

In addition we have caused letters patent to be made for the barons, bearing witness to this security and to the concessions set out above, over the seals of Stephen archbishop of Canterbury, henry archbishop of Dublin, the other bishops named above, and Master Pandulf.

63 IT IS ACCORDINGLY OUR WISh AND COMMAND that the English Church shall be free, and that men in our kingdom shall have and keep all these liberties, rights, and concessions, well and peaceably in their fulness and entirety for them and their heirs, of us and our heirs, in all things and all places for ever.

Both we and the barons have sworn that all this shall be observed in good faith and without deceit. Witness the abovementioned people and many others.

Given by our hand in the meadow that is called Runnymede, between Windsor and Staines, on the fifteenth day of June in the seventeenth year of our reign (i.e. 1215: the new regnal year began on 28 May).

NEAR THIS SPOT
ON THE 20ᵀᴴ NOVEMBER A.D. 1214.
CARDINAL LANGTON & THE BARONS
SWORE AT Sᵀ EDMUND'S ALTAR
THAT THEY WOULD OBTAIN FROM
KING JOHN
THE RATIFICATION OF
MAGNA CHARTA.

The tomb of King John in the chancel of Worcester Cathedral. Contrary to popular supposition, Magna Carta failed at the time to heal the rift between king and barons. John died of dysentery at Newark in 1217 in the course of the continuing civil war.